Great Women of the Old West

by Judy Alter

Content Adviser: Professor Sherry L. Field,
Department of Social Science Education, College of Education,
The University of Georgia

Reading Adviser: Dr. Linda D. Labbo,
Department of Reading Education, College of Education,
The University of Georgia

COMPASS POINT BOOKS

Minneapolis, Minnesota

With love for my husband Bob and to the journeys that lie ahead of us

Compass Point Books
3722 West 50th Street, #115
Minneapolis, MN 55410

Visit Compass Point Books on the Internet at *www.compasspointbooks.com* or e-mail your request
to *custserv@compasspointbooks.com*

Photographs ©: North Wind Picture Archives, cover, 18, 19, 21, 22, 23, 24, 25, 29, 34; Historic
VU/Visuals Unlimited, 4; Denver Public Library/Western History Collection, 5, 7, 8, 9, 10, 11, 12,
13, 14, 15, 16, 31; Hulton Getty/Archive Photos, 6, 35; Stock Montage, 17, 20, 36, 37, 38 (top and
bottom), 39; XNR Productions, Inc., 26; Wyoming Division for Cultural Resources, 27; Kansas
State Historical Society, Topeka, Kansas, 28; The Bancroft Library, University of California,
Berkeley, 33; Reuters/Terry Bochatey/Archive Photos, 40; Wally McNamee/Corbis, 41.

Editors: E. Russell Primm, Emily J. Dolbear, and Deborah Cannarella
Photo Researcher: Svetlana Zhurkina
Photo Selector: Linda S. Koutris
Designer: Bradfordesign, Inc.

Library of Congress Cataloging-in-Publication Data

Alter, Judy, 1938–
   Great women of the Old West / by Judy Alter.
     p. cm. — (We the people)
   Includes bibliographical references and index.
   ISBN 0-7565-0099-0 (lib. bdg.)
     1. Women pioneers—West (U.S.)—History—Juvenile literature. 2. Frontier and pioneer
life—West (U.S.)—Juvenile literature. 3. Indian women—West (U.S.)—History—Juvenile literature. 4. Hispanic American women—West (U.S.)—History—Juvenile literature. 5. Afro-American
women—West (U.S.)—History—Juvenile literature. 6. West (U.S.)—History—Juvenile literature.
[1. Women pioneers. 2. Frontier and pioneer life—West (U.S.) 3. West (U.S.)—Social life and
customs. 4. Women—Biography.] I. Title. II. We the people (Compass Point Books)
   F596 .A44 2001
   9787'.0082—dc21
                                                 00-011016

TABLE OF CONTENTS

SACAGAWEA

The Old West was the land
of American pioneers
during the nineteenth
century. The new
frontier reached from
the Mississippi River
west to the Pacific Ocean,
and from Canada south to
the Mexican border. This vast
region had many different types
of land—mountains, plains, prairies, and deserts.

*The first great women
of the Old West were
American Indians.*

    The region was also home to many different
kinds of women—and all of them helped to shape
its history. The first of these great women were
Native Americans, or American Indians.

4

Sacagawea is probably the most famous American Indian woman of the Old West. In 1804, explorers Meriwether Lewis and William Clark took the young woman with them as their guide. Although she was only about seventeen years old, Sacagawea was a great help to the explorers.

Sacagawea was a Shoshoni Indian.

The Lewis and Clark expedition was searching for a land-and-water route to the Pacific Ocean. Sacagawea, who was a Shoshoni Indian, knew the area well and could find short-cuts. She was also quick to act in times of trouble.

5

Many Indian tribes helped the Lewis and Clark Expedition on its trip through the West.

She saved important papers and supplies when the expedition's boats almost capsized in a river.

The presence of a woman in their group also showed the Indian tribes in the region—the Nez Percé, Flathead, and others—that the explorers traveled in peace. When the Lewis and Clark Expedition reached Shoshoni country (today's states of Idaho and Montana), Sacagawea convinced the

6

Indians to sell Lewis and Clark the horses they needed to cross the Rocky Mountains.

According to one story, Sacagawea lived to be 100 years old. Another story claims that she died from a snakebite when she was twenty-six years old.

More than twenty monuments throughout the West are named for Sacagawea. Her image also appears on the golden dollar first issued by the United States in 2000.

Sacagawea helped the explorers by translating the Shoshoni Indians' words.

INDIAN WOMEN AT WORK AND WAR

Many tribes of American Indians lived in what is now the United States. They did not share one language or one culture. They had different customs and different ways of living.

For example, the Hopi and the Navajo were farmers who lived in villages. The Plains Indians

A Plains Indian camp in the late nineteenth century

A Hopi village in the 1880s

were hunters who often moved their **tepees** from
place to place. The Plains Indian tribes included
the Kiowa, Comanche, Pawnee, Cheyenne, and
Arapaho.

The women in all these tribes had much
in common, however. While the men hunted
for food and fought in battles, the women did

9

After a buffalo hunt, Native American women had much work to do.

everything else. Women planted crops and gather-ed fruits and vegetables. They also gathered wood and cooked meals over open fires. They raised the children, made the clothing, and did whatever else was necessary for daily life.

The women of the Plains tribes took down the tepees when it was time for the tribe to move. When the tribes reached a new location, the women set up the tepees again.

This Salish (Flathead) woman cooks over an open fire in front of her tepee.

11

When the hunters killed buffalo, the women would **tan** the animals' hides. They decorated the hides to make tepee covers. They also made leggings, moccasins, mittens, shirts, and other garments from the buffalo hides. Women decorated the warriors' weapons with porcupine quills and bird feathers.

The Navajo and Hopi women of the Southwest wove clothing from cotton and wool. They **sheared**

A Ute woman stretches an animal hide over the tepee poles.

A Crow woman cleans an animal hide.

the wool off their sheep and spun it into thread. They wove fabric on looms much like those used by the same tribes today. The women of these tribes were also known for their beautiful pottery.

When they were not working, the women visited one another and played games. In one popular game, players moved around a blanket by gaining points. In the center of the blanket was an awl—a stone tool used to work on animal hides. The women threw sticks at the awl to score.

Young girls also played kickball, a simple form of soccer. Most of a young woman's time was spent learning to make **beadwork**, sew, and cook.

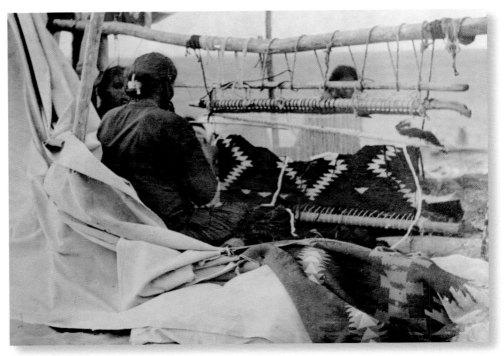

A Navajo woman and girls sit near a loom used for weaving cloth.

14

Snake Indian women play cards.

American Indian women sometimes helped defend their camps and villages.

During battles, the women would watch from a safe distance. If their camp or village was threatened, however, they built barricades of tree branches and soil. According to legend, some women even fought in the battles. Woman Chief, a famous woman warrior, was born a Gros Ventre Indian. She was captured as a child and raised as a member of the Crow people. When she grew up, she led Crow warriors against the Blackfeet Indians. The Crow took seventy horses and two scalps. Woman Chief later led the Crow in a battle against her own relatives, the Gros Ventre, who killed her for revenge.

16

THE SPANISH WOMEN

The Spanish were the first Europeans to reach the Old West. They traveled north from Old Mexico to the lands that are now New Mexico, Texas, and California. The **conquistadors** and priests who came in the sixteenth century were the first to arrive.

Spaniards were the first Europeans to settle what is now the southwestern United States.

17

The conquistadors wanted to claim land and riches for Spain. The priests wanted to convert Native Americans to the Roman Catholic faith. These men did not bring women with them, except for a few servants.

By 1800, the Spanish had settled in Santa Fe (New Mexico), San Antonio (Texas), and parts of California. These settlers brought their families with them.

The oldest house in Santa Fe, New Mexico

18

A Spanish hacienda

There were two groups of Spanish women in the Old West: peasant women and wealthy women. Some peasant women worked for the owners of the large **haciendas** (ranches). Others worked on small family ranches. The wealthy women lived in the haciendas.

19

These large ranches were far apart, so the women were often lonely. Frequent visiting was an important part of their lifestyles. Fandangos and other folk dances also provided social opportunities for the women.

A fandango in California

20

Spanish women followed strict rules about behavior. According to tradition, young men courted young women only through windows. A suitor declared his affection by standing and often singing, outside a young lady's window.

A young girl listens to a boy courting her outside her window.

The boy and girl were allowed to meet only in the presence of a chaperone to ensure proper behavior.

Wealthy women wore layers of rich clothing, often of a dark color, with a traditional Spanish mantilla, or lace shawl, over their heads. Peasant

Spanish women of the Old West wore brightly colored clothes.

women often wore brightly colored cotton skirts and the off-the-shoulder blouses known today as peasant blouses. The influence of the clothing worn by the Spanish and American Indian women of the Old West can still be seen in today's Western-style clothing.

The best-known Spanish woman of the American Old West is La Tules, a gambler who lived in Santa Fe in the early nineteenth century. La Tules was a woman of wealth and social standing. She was often criticized, however, because she ran a business that allowed gambling, smoking, and drinking.

22

CROSSING THE PLAINS

The next group of Europeans to arrive in the American West came from the eastern United States. Mountain men and trappers began to travel west in the 1830s. Like the early Spaniards, these men came to the West alone. A few of them later married American Indian women.

By the mid-1840s, settlers were crossing the prairies in ox-drawn wagons. These men brought their wives and children with them.

The mountain men of the Old West arrived without wives or families.

23

Traveling by covered wagon across the Great Plains

The journey was long and hard. **Covered wagons**—sometimes called prairie schooners— were small and crowded. After the wagon was loaded with the family's household goods, there wasn't much room left for the family.

Women either rode on the wagon, driving the oxen, or walked alongside with their husbands and the older children. Small children were carried or crammed into a corner of the wagon. Mothers had

24

to watch their toddlers constantly to be sure they did not wander away and get lost on the prairie.

The clothes women wore in the East were not suited to life on the trail. Pioneer women wore high-topped boots to protect them from

Women settlers wore plain dresses and strong shoes.

snakebites. They wore bonnets to keep off the sun. Long underwear kept them warm in winter.

These women often had to bathe in dirty river water and had little privacy. They might have used a broken piece of looking glass or a

The Old West with present-day state borders

piece of tin as a mirror. The sun darkened their
skin, and they bleached it with sour milk or
buttermilk to lighten it again. They used
cornstarch as face powder.

26

THE PIONEER WOMEN

Once they arrived in the West, the pioneers had to build their homes. They lived in different kinds of houses depending on where they settled. In the Pacific Northwest, for example, there was plenty of lumber. Settlers there built log cabins. In the Great Plains, where there were no trees, the settlers built sod huts and dugouts. The dugouts were built right into the ground, often in the side of a hill.

A sod house

Everyday life was difficult for pioneer women. They often had to do the backbreaking work of plowing the fields for planting. It was almost impossible to keep their houses clean. The floors were made of dirt! Women in sod huts hung cheesecloth over the beds and stove (if they had a stove) to keep out the dirt and bugs that dropped from the dirt roof.

Dried buffalo droppings—called dung—were used as fuel for cooking.

28

Prairie fires were a danger to settlers' homes.

Pictures from this period show tired-looking women with children clutching their ragged skirts. One famous picture shows a woman with soiled white gloves holding a wheelbarrow. She has been collecting buffalo chips (animal droppings) to use as fuel in her cooking stove.

29

Frontier women lived through many hardships—drought, prairie fires, violent storms, and illnesses for which there were no cures. Their greatest fear, however, was Indian attacks. To the Native Americans, the settlers were invaders who were taking their land. They attacked to drive the settlers away.

Some brave women fought off these attacks. A Texan woman was dipping candles when she heard her son shout that Comanche Indians were approaching the house. The woman hurried her children up to the attic and pulled up the ladder that led from the cabin to the attic. Then, the woman sat at the top of the ladder. She held a kettle of hot wax, ready to pour it on the Comanche who tramped through her cabin.

Some women were taken prisoner by the

30

Indians. The best-known story is told in Fanny Kelly's book, *Narrative of My Captivity among the Sioux Indians*. In 1864, when Fanny was nineteen years old, she left Fort Laramie (Wyoming) with her husband and her stepdaughter, Mary.

This white woman was kidnapped by the Gros Ventre Indians.

They were attacked by 250 Oglala Sioux Indians less than 80 miles (129 kilometers) away from home. Fanny and Mary were captured, and Mary later died.

31

In her captivity, Fanny showed great courage. Once she saved a white woman who was about to be killed because she cried all the time. Another time, Fanny herself was about to be killed for failing to guard a peace pipe. She opened her purse and gave the men all her paper money. The men were so interested in the paper and its value that they began to question Fanny about it—and simply forgot about killing her.

In her book, Fanny wrote that the Sioux called her "Real Woman" because she set an example for how women should behave. Fanny was eventually returned to a white settlement in exchange for three horses and a wagonload of food supplies.

THE AFRICAN-AMERICAN WOMEN

Biddy Mason

Many African-American women traveled west— often as slaves. Only a few of these women were able to leave any record of their lives.

Biddy Mason was a slave who traveled from Mississippi to California in 1851. She drove sheep behind the wagon her owner traveled in. In 1854, when Biddy's owner wanted to leave California, she talked to the local sheriff. She convinced him to issue a writ, or order, that would keep her owner from taking Biddy and her three daughters out of the state.

33

In 1856, Biddy won her freedom in the courts. In the 1860s, she began buying real estate. She soon became wealthy enough to help other black families.

After the Civil War ended in 1865, many more settlers arrived in the West. Some were Southerners who had lost their homes in the war.

Homesteaders building a log cabin

34

A general store and post office on an Indian reservation in New Mexico, about 1885

These people were drawn to the West by the promise of land on which they could build new homes. The government was offering homesteads—large parcels of land—to anyone who would settle the land and live on it for five years.

The West also became a safer place for settlers in the late 1800s. Between 1865 and 1900, almost the entire American Indian population was confined to **reservations**. What the Native Americans feared most had actually happened: The settlers had taken their land.

35

MAKING NEW LIVES

Once settled in the West, women tried to create lives like those they had left behind in Illinois and Kentucky, Missouri and New York. They wore the clothing they had brought with them from the East. They planted gardens and established schools, churches, study groups, and charitable organizations.

Pioneers began to order much of what they needed from catalogs sent by Sears, Roebuck and Company and other large stores.

By the 1890s, women in the West were receiving catalogs from large stores, such as Sears, Roebuck and Company and Montgomery Ward.

36

These catalogs allowed the women to order the clothes and household goods they could not get in their western communities.

By 1900, the West had towns, farms, ranches, fences, and civilization. In many ways, it began to look like the rest of the United States.

Many women traveled west by themselves. About 15 percent of the homesteaders were un-married or widowed women. The West gave women freedom they didn't have anywhere else.

Lucille Mulhall (left)

37

Annie Oakley

Many women took on work that was usually done by men.

Georgia Arbuckle Fix practiced medicine in western Nebraska. She rode horseback over more than 30 miles (48 km) of prairie to see her patients. Mattie Castner, who was born into slavery, became a wealthy landowner and respected citizen of Montana. Nellie Cashman was a restaurant owner and miner. She traveled by steamer and dogsled to save miners who were dying from a disease called **scurvy** in a remote mining camp.

Carry Nation

38

THE SPIRIT OF THE OLD WEST

Throughout history, the American West has produced many great women. All of them had the strong, independent spirit that the West is still known for. Among the most famous of these women were cowgirl Lucille Mulhall, sharpshooter Annie Oakley, outlaw Belle Starr, reformer Carry Nation, and author Laura Ingalls Wilder.

Wyoming women were the first females in America to receive the right to vote.

Ann Richards

Esther Morris of Wyoming was another great woman of the West. During the mid-nineteenth century, she worked hard for woman suffrage—the right to vote. She convinced a lawmaker to introduce a bill that would grant women several rights. If passed, the bill would give women such privileges as the right to vote, to own property, to earn money and keep it, to serve on juries, and to be guardians of minor children.

Because of Esther Morris's work, Wyoming became the first state to give American women the right to vote. Esther Morris voted for the first time in 1869. In 1870, she became the world's first female justice of the peace. In 1892, she was a delegate to the National Republican Convention.

A century later, the legacy of the women of the Old West has been passed to many others: Wilma Mankiller became president of the Cherokee Nation; Ann Richards became governor of Texas; and Sandra Day O'Connor sits on the U.S. Supreme Court. Although the days of the Old West are gone, the spirit of the American West lives on in the great women who still shape our country today.

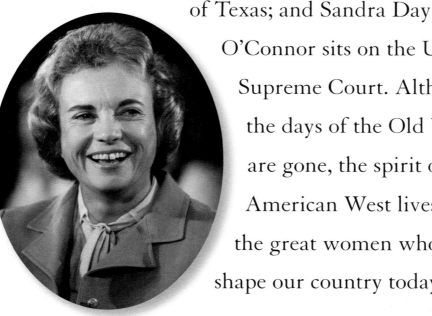

Sandra Day O'Connor

41

GLOSSARY

beadwork—decorations made by sewing beads onto fabric

conquistadors—Spanish military leaders of the sixteenth century who claimed lands in the Americas for the Spanish king

covered wagons—wagons covered with a high, canvas top in which many of the pioneers traveled west

dugout—a shelter about the size of a small room dug into a hillside

hacienda—the Spanish name for a large ranch or estate; the main house on the estate

reservations—tracts of land set aside by a government for a specific purpose

scurvy—a disease marked by swollen and bleeding gums. It is caused by a lack of enough fresh fruits and vegetables

shear—to cut the fleece off a sheep

tan—to make animal hide into leather

tepees—cone-shaped tents used by the Plains Indians, made of buffalo hide and three tall poles

42

DID YOU KNOW?

- Sharpshooter Annie Oakley was a member of Buffalo Bill's Wild West show. She could shoot a playing card a dozen times with her rifle before the card hit the ground.

- Laura Ingalls Wilder and her family traveled by covered wagon through parts of what is now the Midwest. She wrote many books based on her childhood, including *Little House on the Prairie* and *Little Town on the Prairie*.

- Wyoming was the first U.S. state to give women the right to vote.

IMPORTANT DATES

Timeline

1527 — Cabeza de Vaca sails from Spain to the New World. He is the first Spanish conquistador to explore the American West.

1804– 1806 — The Lewis and Clark Expedition maps a route across the northwestern United States and the Rocky Mountains to the Pacific Ocean.

1848 — Gold is discovered in California, bringing the first wave of settlers into Spanish California.

1865 — The Civil War ends, and more settlers travel to the West.

1876 — The Sioux and several other tribes defeat Lieutenant Colonel George Armstrong Custer at the Battle of the Little Bighorn. After this final victory, almost all Native Americans are sent to reservations, clearing the way for more settlement of the West.

1900 — The West is settled with cities, towns, farms, and ranches. The settlers have claimed the lands that once were occupied by American Indians and established a new lifestyle in the West.

IMPORTANT PEOPLE

SACAGAWEA

(1786?–1812), *the young Shoshoni Indian woman who served as a guide to Lewis and Clark on their famous expedition across the northwestern United States.*

FANNY KELLY

(1845– ?), *a young woman who was captured by Sioux Indians. Later rescued, she wrote about her experience in* Narrative of My Captivity among the Sioux Indians.

WILMA PEARL MANKILLER

(1945–), *Cherokee Native American leader and the first woman chief of a large tribe*

ESTHER HOBART MORRIS

(1814–1902), *Wyoming resident who became the first woman to cast a vote in the United States and the first female justice of the peace*

CARRY AMELIA MOORE NATION

(1846–1911), *teacher and social reformer who is best known for destroying saloons with an ax in her efforts to outlaw alcohol*

LAURA INGALLS WILDER

(1867–1957), *author of children's books based on her childhood experiences on the American frontier*

WANT TO KNOW MORE?

At the Library

Alter, Judy. *Extraordinary Women of the American West*. Danbury, Conn.: Children's Press, 1999.

Anderson, Joan. *Spanish Pioneers of the Southwest*. New York: E. P. Dutton, 1989.

Flynn, Jean. *Annie Oakley: Legendary Sharpshooter*. Berkeley Heights, N.J.: Enslow Publications, 1998.

Katz, William Loren. *Black Women of the Old West*. New York: Atheneum, 1995.

McLoone, Margo (Margo McLoone-Basta). *Women Explorers in North and South America: Nellie Cashman, Annie Peck, Ynes Mexia, Blair Niles, Violet Cissy Marcks*. Mankato, Minn.: Capstone Press, 1997.

Wilson, Ellen Janet Cameron. *Annie Oakley: Young Markswoman*. New York: Aladdin Paperbacks, 1989.

On the Web

Women Writing the West

http://www.womenwritingthewest.org

A nonprofit organization supporting the work of authors, including children's authors, who write about women's experiences in the West

Women of the West Museum

http://www.wowmuseum.org

For stories and artwork about and by women of the West, recommended books, a "story quilt," and a chance for visitors to the site to submit their own stories

National Cowgirl Museum & Hall of Fame

http://www.cowgirl.net

A Web site that honors pioneer women of the West, including cowgirls, ranch women, teachers, writers, artists, and entertainers

Through the Mail

Women of the West Museum

4001 Discovery Drive

Boulder, CO 80303

303/541-1000

For information about the many women who helped shape the West

On the Road

The National Cowgirl Museum and Hall of Fame and Western Heritage Center

111 West Fourth Street, Suite 300

Fort Worth, TX 76102

817/336-4475

Features hands-on exhibits, theater presentations, photographs, and exhibits about the early years of women's professional rodeo, Western art, and famous women of the West, including Sacagawea and Laura Ingalls Wilder

INDEX

About the Author

Judy Alter is the author of nearly thirty books, both fiction and nonfiction, many of them about women in the American West. She believes that the Western experience shaped women's lives in a very different way from the lives of women in the East.

Her nonfiction books for young readers include *The Santa Fe Trail, Extraordinary Women of the American West, Rodeo: The Best Show on Dirt, Sam Houston, Mapping the American West*, and others.

Judy Alter is the director of a small university publishing division. She has four children—all grown—two cats, and a large dog. Her hobbies include cooking, reading, and gardening.